ANDREW JACKSON

Seventh President of the United States, Andrew Jackson was a fighter all his life. As a young boy barely in his teens, he fought in the Revolutionary War. He then struggled hard to become a lawyer. With the War of 1812 Andrew Jackson fought again and soon he was made a hero for his part in the victory at New Orleans. He was so tough that he earned the nickname Old Hickory. Old Hickory was loved by the people, the backwoodsmen and the frontiersmen. They sent him to Congress and soon elected him President of the country. In this easy-to-read biography you will learn about Andrew Jackson, the people's President.

ANDREW
JACKSON

By Patricia Miles Martin

Illustrated by Salem Tamer

G. P. Putnam's Sons   New York

For Rosemary Wallace

Published simultaneously in the Dominion of
Canada by Longmans Canada Limited, Toronto
Library of Congress Catalog Card Number: 66-10256
PRINTED IN THE UNITED STATES OF AMERICA
07209

ANDREW JACKSON

In the year of 1767, a boy was born on the frontier. He was born in a log cabin in the Waxhaws, between North and South Carolina.

This boy, Andrew Jackson, would one day be President of the United States.

Andrew Jackson never knew his father, for his father died before Andrew was born.

When Andrew was five years old, he learned to write his letters. With a stick, he wrote them on the ground under the hickory trees. Soon he knew how to read.

Andrew grew tall and strong.
He was quick to anger and as
quick to fight.

On the frontier, a man had to watch for Indians. No man went outdoors without taking his rifle with him.

And like all frontier boys, Andrew knew how to use a rifle.

He learned how to take care of himself.

Soon, everyone in the Waxhaws knew him as that fighting, red-haired Jackson boy.

He was nine years old when the Colonies said they would no longer belong to England.

When news of this Declaration reached the Waxhaws, the frontiersmen came to hear about it.

They came from far and near.
Andrew read this long Declaration
of Independence, and the men
listened.

War with England followed.

Four years went by before this war came to the Waxhaws where Andrew lived. Andrew joined the American forces.

The captain gave him a horse and a pistol.

16

A year later, Andrew and his
brother, Robert, were taken
prisoners by the English. The
prisoners were forced to walk many
miles to a prison camp.

In the prison with Andrew were
frontiersmen and backwoodsmen.

Many of these men had been shot
and needed care. Andrew saw them
die.

His two brothers died in this war.
And while his mother was caring
for the sick, she too died.

Andrew was alone.

After the fighting was over,
Andrew rode north. He stopped in
the village of Salisbury in North
Carolina. There he stayed for two
years while he learned about the
law. He became a lawyer.

At this time, men were going west to the land that lay over the mountains. Andrew Jackson went with them.

He rode a strong horse, and
carried his books tied on behind his
saddle. It was autumn when he
reached Nashville.

In Nashville, Andrew Jackson
worked hard, and he played hard.
He was still quick to anger and
as quick to fight.

Once, he became angry and
challenged another lawyer to a duel.
Their friends talked to them.
They said it was not wise to fight
a duel. They told each man he
should not kill the other.

The hour came to fight.

The two men were ready, their
pistols in their hands. When they
heard the word "Fire," each man
shot his pistol into the air.

In Nashville, Andrew Jackson met
the woman who became his wife,
Rachel Robards.

He bought land near the
Mississippi River. Here in a strong,
log house, he and Rachel lived
happily.

Andrew Jackson was a busy man.
He was a farmer. He was a lawyer.
He was away from home much
of the time. When he was away,
Rachel watched over the farm. And
her work was well done.

Andrew Jackson was well known
in the territory where he worked.

When the territory became a
state, he was its first Congressman.

He went at once to the Capitol.
His coat was old and his hair was
tied with an eelskin. Proudly he
took his place with the well-dressed
Congressmen from the states in the
East.

Andrew Jackson was well liked in Tennessee.

He was Senator for the people of Tennessee.

He was Judge of their Supreme Court.

He was General of the Tennessee Militia. Under his command were 2,500 men who were ready to fight.

1375987

One day in June of 1812, a rider galloped into town. He brought word that the United States and England were again at war. They were at war on sea, as well as on land.

The Creek Indians had joined the English in this war.

General Jackson led the militia through the woods, fighting Creeks along the way.

At last, these Indians were caught at Horseshoe Bend. The Creeks fought there until they were killed.

The men of the militia said of Andrew Jackson, "He is as tough as hickory." And "Hickory" he was called from this day on.

General Jackson heard that a great English army was on its way to New Orleans. He led his men there.

After a hard fight that lasted many days, they won the Battle of New Orleans.

The happy people of New Orleans shouted and cheered.

Drums rolled, and there was dancing in the streets.

The war of 1812 was over, and Andrew Jackson was a hero.

He was the best-loved man in the United States.

After happy months at home with Rachel, again Andrew Jackson led his militia. Again there was Indian trouble. The trouble was with the Seminoles.

Friendly Seminoles in Georgia wanted to keep land which was theirs by treaty. But frontiersmen wanted the land.

Andrew Jackson believed that Indians had no right to land that frontiersmen wanted.

The Seminoles went on the war path.

General Jackson led his men to Georgia to fight the Indians.

The Seminoles moved on, into Florida, which was then owned by Spain.

General Jackson wanted to follow the Indians and take Florida by force.

He wrote to the President of the United States asking for this right.

President Monroe did not answer.

General Jackson did not wait long, but went to Florida. Without hearing from the President, he led his men through swamps, hunting for the Seminoles.

At last, angry at not finding them, he went straight to the capital of Florida. He took the city without a fight.

Because he had taken the capital of Florida, President Monroe was not pleased with Andrew Jackson.

Spain was not pleased.

But the people of the United States were pleased. The frontiersmen and the backwoodsmen were pleased. They loved Andrew Jackson for what he had done.

A short time after this, Spain sold
Florida to the United States.
President Monroe then made
Andrew Jackson Governor of the
Territory of Florida.

It was not long before his friends
in Tennessee talked about electing
"Old Hickory" President of the
United States.

People from the states in the East
talked about electing other men.

Andrew Jackson lost this election.

At once he started to get ready
for the next election.

He talked to people everywhere.
And the people did not forget the
man who had fought the Indians.
They did not forget the hero of
New Orleans.

He won the next election.

Andrew and Rachel talked about
the time when they would go to
Washington together. A few months
before Andrew Jackson would be

made President, Rachel died.

She was buried in their own
beautiful garden.

Again, Andrew Jackson was alone.

One day in March of 1829, he became the seventh President of the United States.

A great crowd of happy men cheered the new President.

President Jackson rode to the White House.

The crowd followed. It pushed its
way into the White House with
him. The men were laughing and
shoving. They were cheering the
man they had elected, Andrew
Jackson, the best-loved man in the
United States.

While Andrew Jackson was President, there was trouble between the Federal Government and the state government of South Carolina.

South Carolina held that states had the right to make their own laws. The people of South Carolina said they would not accept the laws of the Federal Government. They said they would withdraw from the United States if the Federal Government used force against them.

President Jackson was angry.

Quickly, he moved against South Carolina.

Ships and men were made ready for war.

The President made a
Proclamation. In this Proclamation,
he said that no state had a right to
withdraw from the Union.

South Carolina accepted the laws
of the Federal Government, and did
not withdraw from the Union.

The President's popularity was
greater than before.

Andrew Jackson was President of the United States for eight years.

At the end of that time, he spoke to the people. He told them he was ready to go home. He knew that his life would soon be over, but he was thankful that his life had been lived in a land of liberty.

Andrew Jackson, gentleman and fighting frontiersman, died in June of 1845.

He was one of the great Presidents. He was a man who worked for the good of the people he represented, the men from the backwoods, the men from the wide frontiers.

Key Words

accepted

anger

born

between

backwoods-man-men

buried

challenged

cheer-ed-ing

command

died

duel

eelskin

elect-ing-ion

frontier-s-man-men

force-s

fought

hickory

hero

joined

kill

law, lawyer

life

liberty

pistol-s

popularity

prison-ers

rifle

rough

represented

shoving

state-s

swamps

treaty

territory

tough

withdraw

won

war

The Author

PATRICIA MILES MARTIN and her husband live in San Mateo, California, where she writes six days a week in a pantry-turned-office. She describes herself as a "compulsive writer," having had her first poem accepted by a newspaper in Monette, Missouri, when she was seven years old. Now she reviews children's books in several well-known newspapers throughout the United States.

Mrs. Martin wrote poetry until 1957, and then started writing for young people. She has been most successful and has more than a dozen books to her credit.

The Artist

SALEM TAMER has been making pictures as far back as he can remember, but his formal art training includes studies at Vesper George School in Boston and the Art Students League of New York. His illustrations for books and magazines, his advertising art, book jackets, and industrial publications, include more than one prize-winning design. As art director of the Mergenthaler Linotype Company, he won recognition and numerous AIGA awards in design and typography.

Mr. Tamer and his family live on Long Island.